Home

Home

Emily Critchley

Home by Emily Critchley
Published by Prototype in 2021

The right of Emily Critchley to be identified as author of this work has been asserted in accordance with Section 77 of the UK Copyright, Designs and Patents Act 1988.

Copyright © Emily Critchley 2021
All rights reserved

No part of this publication may be reproduced, stored in a retrieval system, or transmitted, in any form or by any means, electronic, mechanical, photocopying, recording or otherwise, without the prior permission of the publishers. A CIP record for this book is available from the British Library.

Design by Theo Inglis
Typeset in Garamond Classico
Printed in the UK by TJ Books

ISBN 978-1-913513-08-5

( )   (   )
 p   prototype

(type 1 – poetry)
www.prototypepublishing.co.uk
@prototypepubs

prototype publishing
71 oriel road
london e9 5sg
uk

Will you be good towards
these animals of unease
I can just about call them home.

–Denise Riley, 'A Shortened Set'

For my daughter, always.

With love & gratitude to Daniel Krähmer, Alex Goodall,
Catherine Wagner, Rosie Šnajdr, Denise Riley,
John Wilkinson, Ágnes Lehóczky, Elizabeth-Jane Burnett,
Charis Hanning, Sascha Akhtar, James Goodwin,
Marianne Morris, Zoë Skoulding, Rachael Allen,
Jack Underwood, Peter Hobbs, Lydia Wilson, John Hall,
Peter Riley, Nathan Hamilton, Ed Doegar, Rachael Boast,
Andy Ching, SJ Fowler, Aaron Kent, Eric Powell,
Gareth Prior, Alex Pheby, Nuar Alsadir, Khadeja Ishaq,
The Rialto, *The Learned Pig*, *Granta*, *The Chicago Review*,
Cambridge Literary Review, Poetry Translation Centre,
PN Review, *Hotel Magazine*, *Fortnightly Review*,
the *Oxford English Journal*, English PEN and of course
my publisher, Jess.

Contents

After E.D. – 9

Part I
Tonight – 13
Little Death Waltz – 14
Caught – 16
There [Not There] – 17
Ghost-Language [or Die Sprache spricht] – 18
And We Make A Polis – 20
Still News – 22
Please Don't Leave – 24
That Nested Hierarchy [of Soul Functions qua Activities] – 25
In Memory W.S. Graham – 30
Home – 31
It's Not Personal – 33

Part II
Error Term – 39
Für du [sic.] – 40
All We Have Are Metonyms – 42
Hello Again – 43
Here – 44
In The Family Box – 45
The Verdict – 46
Room On Fire – 48
5.11.18 – 50
No Title [Language is the House of Being] – 51
Two Lessons – 52
I'm Walking Away From You Now And I Can't – 54
Bluebottles – 55
Victory Blossoms – 56
Out of Joint – 57
Snow – 58

After E.D.

Because we would not heed the Best –
The Worst came unawares.
He laughed to see our little lives –
He cared not for our cares –

You Fools – He said – You had the Day!
Your god had made you gods –
And all you had to do was Love –
And all the Rest was Yours.

But Ego would as Ego does
Prevent the Better News
From taking Root – in Gratitude
& Shining forth as Flow'rs –

Now is it Long Ago – our Prime –
& wintering we see
too late – what spring we held – too light
and so Unspiritually.

Part I

Tonight
for Marianne Morris

Everything is a part of everything that is a part of everything else.
And any decision is like a huge moon
tossed from the top of a great hill. It gathers speed
in direct proportion to height,
taking each prisoner down with it.
It & the tides.

And when we were younger, things dropped
were as stones into that ocean. But now,
just as the moon gapes, we have run out
of ideas.

Everything is a part of everything else that is a part
of nothing. The moon moves;
cuts its teeth
on our regretful actions. Like that time
we made bombs out of love. Live
bombs sent to rip us with.
She grew, O,
into a strong one.

And I keep pointing out the moon –
part of a shared
sky – while you keep running from the moon,
a part of every other
possibility. Still
if you can see it – she,
above,
craning her neck for a better view –
we must be thinking of the same place then.

Little Death Waltz

In the heart of hearths there is her – she wolf –
    who – linking arms with your first-born –
    who – shedding dresses, crossing
breeds with –
    leading him on to
    outrageous death waltz,
allowing outside
wildly in with laughter.

Who ought to be ashamed
who – someone should fetch grandpa's gun.

Lines around this
hearth-polis –
    snares and mountain ranges
    tongues of many different knives of colours
for (fun for) law & order.
Who – will howl for her please?
Who – leave a plate of milk at the border?

O she in wolf's clothing –
no Mother nor Father –
that wildness is:
brazen wound dancer.

O we are no waltzing sheep who
does she think she is?

Little death waltz, little death waltz –
    prescient of death
    and self-fulfilling like foundations

that we dig
to be filled up
with grave-water.

Who will snatch her child up in her mouth –
who bear her miles from here.

She – animal – will never speak / can never
tell of horrors done to it,
only sing at moonlight
where traps she knows are best laid
       [who will cry for her at the border?]
       and strangely dance.

Hurling from that rock
        only to be caught
                by a partridge of the ground
                        actually a passing peacock

      for John Hall

There [Not There]
for Elizabeth-Jane Burnett

Call the facts the facts. Then call a spade a tool for eating rose tints with.
Call the coincidence of the garden subjugation of a beautiful effacement.
Call the presiding angel of that hour:
memory of a lost pathway,
shelter of a tranquil evening,
a plea – perhaps our lost biophilia.
Call the eye catching on it, anthers feasting, its own reward.

If you remember not yourself, but others,
there will always be someone to be thankful to.
If you remember not yourself, but others, there will always be someone
to put before your own myopia. If you remember not yourself,
but others, no one can accuse you of acting out
the usual
multivalent
trauma.

Call each present passing through the coincidence of that garden
a longed returning to our lost bones in the garden,
each delicate, momentary fossil.
Call the recollection of a time you thought you could not bear, but did
      bear,
conditional victory over the sabotaging spirit.
And not a victory that need well up some other way,
destroy some other accidental happiness.

If you step into the cool shade of the moment going, there is still a nearness
that can comfort;
reviving glance, perhaps, of coral roses
you yourself once planted there.

Ghost-Language [or Die Sprache spricht]

Now that she & you & he & her & him & they & his & yours & ours
        are taken care of,
I can attend to
bruised ghosts of language, sepia-edged, neverfleeing.

                                      All weapons point the same way
    yet I too have lived with hostages
        and, silver-tongued, I found a way to say,
            to shut up my self, to
      stay with them. Take the girl but leave
the ghost-skin
to play.

Then she & you & he & her & him & they & all incidentals.

Listen to the human's rib. I mean listen to his heart. Lying
not by intention but distraction. Both beating down
the same.

                And when you go you should move silence,
free a clearing to the door.

                And when you go you should take the objects
– though they bring bad juju.

                And when you go, find someone new
                                  to house presence,

making more, releasing ghost-time:
> little ghosts that haunt the golden meadows or hide
> > out in plain
> sight   just

off   the
beaten track.

When you go, find someone new to love. Let her speak her language for a change. Let her make you listen. Make sure to listen.

And We Make A Polis
for Theodoros Chiotis

Politics from πολιτικός
of, for, or relating to the people
like poetry, or family
like good or bad leaders

all segments of society
involving power and authority
as who sings most fairly
or who thinks most rightly

(like family or poetry)
from out of the polis
this 'this' of the people.

Property is my poem
given back to me
the right to my re-write
the little, not the main

though to exercise my right
sometimes goes against my people
in the past, future, present
so the growth of opinion
(like the history of knowledge
which is the history of property)
is institutional structure
is protection in numbers

is exclusionary as anything
is invisible as we're in it.

(The more man becomes knowledgeable
more world he owns,
the more man becomes knowledgeable
more world he owes.)

Mini history
I sing 'you liar
You liar' I sing.

From wildlife to husbandry
from farmhold to sanctuary
staving off vulnerability
man achieves property

From wildlife to husbandry
from farmhold to property
to prop up the symmetry
woman slots in this hierarchy

and for ('the common') good.

Still News

Can do maybe a new day apart from this momentous shift in light which
like at one time you only have a certain share of lives to
use up / smash clean
                 / best not imprint them all at once
when apocalyptic black's so in
this season, and in the middle of this
    big bad month
(exactly 100 days later)
   I find (even in my dreams)
I'm still sporting the same
shade, this so predictable
in this
        retro dread, which I'll wear like a dress each Sunday
        or so except when I'm not
pregnant, but today is Sunday and I don't know
what I should be
      stupid, OK.

I want everybody else judged for being stupid too.
      You for not reading
the news before you eat it; it for pushing
abject-porn over the truth; and anyone
for gunning people down
       especially the children. If this poem came with firepower
I would eat
their
hearts out
in the marketplace.
              Is that intolerant to hate intolerance?
Is that it not OK?
      'If love is this hard…'[*] every time should be the last.

After this I'm done.
                    But is it too late for that? Yes is it too late for that.

News leave me, and the pity,
& especially O self-congratulating
poetry.

The Internet can fuck itself with its electro-eyes that try
buying its way
into our natural core.   Well what is wrong with
                                     turning new leaves

in books I'd like to know (except
         they kill the trees
         to make 'em).

*Marianne Morris

Please Don't Leave

either side there is no
matter / when you are
away you are
away / the small child
still forgets itself / still
picks up (where it left
from school or) face it
in a sun or
puddle / how do we
begin? The clock frames our
concern / & when
you are away
you are away / This view
's a loop / & thinking-feeling:
shadow-play /
of light
   against
the cave. / How long it's been
that sometimes I forget
the small child waits /
etc.

& when you are / away
I have you still. I burden
you a heart / will always.

That Nested Hierarchy [of Soul Functions qua Activities]
for Gareth Prior

It being Saturday & any way you view it it is expensive,
emotionally, this, a Saturday, & looking round for something more
than Saturday to come keep me warm. My memories,
alone with them, are nothing but my thoughts & I,
but then the dream,
it woke me: back when you were interesting
   to me,
    & I was interesting to you,
& now there's no way back against that wall because I guess that what I'm saying is the
dream has shot itself into a wall because

there can be no dreaming without equality.

I must remember you at one time
(like a complimentary pen on making the inquiry
in writing) if I'm not to overwhelm myself
with animus of virtue
– when I do, do I, admire such
consistency of thought greatly.

O Aristotle, where are you tonight.
   You're probably the only one
that ever felt potentially, since the form is all that matters, since the 'this' is still the soul
of living (not its shape or anything so base as argued out of living) just:
    those grades of Actuality v. Potentiality.

You called this knowing & attending, also sleeping v. awaking, but did not clarify,
importantly, till I turned to you & asked you saying:

There are so many different versions, A!
Of both potentiality and actuality.

How can you keep them separate in your head? You being only human / having grammatical knowledge / & attending
>   to so many other things!

To which he did reply, saying he'd been mistaken in the strictness of his separateness. In fact:
a knower is as someone with potential a) to know something
but has no actual knowledge (like a rock or complimentary   pen)
A knower in sense b) is one with actual knowledge, for example, she may   know that it is ungrammatical to say 'with him and I', even though
she is not thinking that at any time. A knower in sense c) is exercising   knowledge, for example, she thinks 'that's ungrammatical' when she hears someone say 'with him and I'
or 'fuck the complimentary pen, it [–] that [–] a dream pen, now you're right back to where you –'

a) first potentiality
b) second potentiality = first actuality
c) second actuality

But that was not the knowing she & I were both after.

The actual knowing was potentiality
to think certain thoughts / perform certain actions – *out* of the frame of certain categorisations.

So describing three separate knowers was never going to work
for you (even were you to be a silent knower
with only the potential to speak ((French)). The child who does not act that expectation always wins the pen; life being a concatenation
of unreasonable patterns).

But Aristotle,
do you still remember when you used the *actuality* example

in your definition of the soul, it being so unlike the pen because so natural & too
potentially ideal to write that to let go?
If soul equals the capacity – then what to do?

& Aristotle did reply: I do;
a living thing's soul *is*
its capacity to do those things
that are most general of living beings.
Never to let go
of that which is most natural to you…
True beauty is not just potential,
your capacity must match your action, you must:

a) self-nourish
b) grow
c) decay
d) move & rest (in respect of place)
e) perceive
f) intellect

You were not that she, born like a child (unlike a pen), purely
for potential, but your intellect becomes you
as a living being. The soul is what is.
Movement will come after.

A nested hierarchy of functions shows itself to me now in the light of acting life. It is:

a) nutritive soul (plants, all animals, human beings)
b) sensitive soul (plants, all animals, human beings)
c) rational soul (plants? all animals? human beings?)

Anything that's 'higher level' (soul) has also 'lower' functions.
We know now trees communicate with earth worms. Animals
not only do that, but they self-protect. So shall she too,

as well as reason.

Yet can the soul move
independently
of
body
or only
if you still believe
in what comes after?

Plato, as we know, thought this unadulterated:
... the soul does not exist without a body and yet is not itself a kind of body. For it is not a body, but something which belongs to a body, and for this reason exists in a body, and in a body of such-and-such a kind ...

Yet is the material not separable from form but only when it comes to intellect?

O, A, don't throw me to the vagueness of the general picture!

To which he thus: The picture stays.
It isn't like it was for Descartes.

a) there is no inner / outer contrast. The soul is not an inner viewer,
in direct contact only with its own perceptions / other
psychic states, having to infer the existence of a body and 'external' world.
b) The soul is not an independently existing substance. It is **capacity**, & not the thing
that has capacity. It isn't **separable**.
c) Yet soul has little to do with personal identity / individuality. No reason to think
that one soul differs in any important respect from any other soul. The form
of one being is the same as that of any other.
There is, in this sense, only **soul**, not souls. You and I have different souls
because we're different compounds: form and matter. Different bodies animated by the same
set of capacities, by the same (kind of) soul.

And there we left it, on that puzzling equivalence, & there I went to bed.
And my sleep was not a composite of head *or* body but a thing comparable
to afterlife, a peaceful thing, requiring nothing of my mind or thought or movement
but merely the sweet memory of life.
Potential of a sunset in a sunrise.
Not bounded by specific form, but part of the totality of soul, & also thus quite able
to exist or wake or sleep or dream as one.

In Memory W.S. Graham
for Rachael, Andy & Nathan

It's late. Call off the knives of language subtly
drawn, funereal. Take significance
with you. Each chosen moment, each

abject tender thing, wound tight
& hurt across the dark, that whitens naked
with dawn. Don't drive into that

rhyme knowing what you know:
how it will all end. The story's not
yet straight with me & lyric I

's become unfashionable again. Or we
have borne too much not to go on.
Each singing choice, each incisive error

could have been different & we know it,
we, who wanted that alive or dead,
but to be real. Or we have come too

far not to give in. And feelings
aren't that way inclined, aren't natural
phenomena. Yes but they are.

Now not one edge left to bleed you with?
Probably it doesn't matter.
Probably the heart's a free-flowing

instrument, impulsive place, directionless.
And now that's hardly occurred,
now you, the text, can all agree on nothing.

Home
for Rachael Allen

I needed a home
so I put you in it.
I put me in it. Scientific –
like an argument
about climate
change. It's the apocalypse,
dummy!
Small rescue boat:
no nuclear warhead,
nothing to see here.
But no peace
at any price
        either.

Being entwined
is such a weird animal!
Sniffing about the place, always
peeing in the same cupboard.
I've told you how many
times not to
but look you've told me
not to –
look my
pointing my gun
        again.

And now the dinner that is
burning. And the earth that is
warming. And apocalypse.
And.

Listen to the ice breaking
are you there. Listen
to the world beneath our feet
duck duck bear.
      Are you there.

Now carrying around heartache
like a second baby,
I will check myself
in to the nearest
equanimity clinic,
sail out
at the first available
promise. Need
a complete detox,
molecular fix,
to understand life,
how to possibly
live in it / break it
      to my daughter.

It's Not Personal
for Ellie Butler & her sister

Born not into this world, but entangled,
impact hardest hit on landing – and he knew
she knew she was a punching bag because her mother
had before her, and her sister, and there were the exes
before that, now strewing tears on daytime television,
and the public stranglings and the pregnant girlfriend
and the retinal haemorrhages and the burns on her fingers
and her forehead (at five weeks) and the little broken arm
and exoneration from the judge and incredulity from everyone.

Trouble is she had no say because *she was only five years old.*

And although several key professionals engaged *purposefully,
directly*, there is a general lack of focus on the child
or on her sister *as individuals and their wishes,
feelings and characters do not feature strongly*
because she was only five years old – the other even younger –
inchoate human beings that never really counted
among the stinging branches and the scalding currents,
the expert testimonies and the legal wranglings. And we know,
have heard it said, how important it is for kids
to be with their parents: that special bond, those precious rights,
the swirling currents – impact of which will be referred to later.

Because *now the child is dead; she had her head bashed in.*

All *narrative and professional attention is paid*
[following a state apology] to *the say-so of her* [grown-up] *parents*.
The child – she knew and *begged* not to be taken
back to 'the bad house' – has come and gone.

Brief promise of a human being petrified
in tears who stumbled, briefly, into the dark fray
of familial love that spins about the centre of this world /
stamps its expert seal on everything and knows,
she knew, we all know how it happened, how it never should,
and how it will again.

Part II

Error Term

for Zoë Skoulding

> '*The border you taped off is crooked I'll say.*'
> – Christie Ann Reynolds

If we draw a straight line – the straightest possible – between, say, the economy & ecology, the reservoir & the road, there will always be this error term. Some people (me) say you can't calculate the incalculable. You (you) say we cannot not. Whenever there's frustration at an exaggeration, that's what I / you mean. Measuring physical variables & outputs, for instance, temperature & pressure. Then you want to measure. Maybe over 100 days, every day. So you will make measurement errors. Sometimes you measure the same pressure & it will result in a different temperature. Sometimes the road to any wilderness will not be straight. The border might swerve (agonistically).[*] Any non-systematic measurement errors should not be part of the underlying relation, however, for instance, between pressure & temperature. Because pressure & temperature. But if you measure every day (every day) you (I) make small errors, and this should not confound (one's) findings.

---

[*] 'the agonistic power to swerve minds out of gender/genre-normative geometries of attention.'
– Joan Retallack

Für du [sic.]

In Berlin you will be good at forgetting,
you already promised me. And there are
hundreds of girls to be checked out by
& a thousand spilled birds to cry over.

In Bonn your position's secured.
It is not too much to expect, with other
guildsmen who understand the value
of little girl studenten too late,

all made up in their musischness. Though
their minds are less likely to be true or
at least undecided. In Swabia the waters
do run clear. We are not sure if this

lends itself to a name and will ignore
the topic till later. In London there is one
to say du du
do und do. There is

a chink of dancing to let music in.
Such clear vibrations on Eighth Street
that in New York you can get felled
by a man just for forgetting (though

you should never try). And where
you grew up (just now) the forests
have much more value than we could decide
to remember or waltz to.

They only obscure
what we didn't see
(till now) in our
Baroque restlessness.

All We Have Are Metonyms

I won't set this poem
in some pastoral beauty

despite flashy autumn
crowing about its colours

each one a place-holder
because *all we have left*

are metonyms
having seen too much

of only the beginning
then skip forward

to a natural entropy
our shaking hands, parting

fine by both, agreed by longed for
'the security of home'

that simple smiling sentence
of the bridge, that utter flood

& other complexities
like this for instance

when we cut out all the things
that speak us wrongly. Do what

ever with the rest. When
we don't cut out all the things –

what, can I ask, is left

Hello Again [after Hugh Sykes Davies]
for Mahvash Sabet & SJ Fowler

In outspoken wakefulness, where the heart has collected, pooled its weary
for a moment / is there a melting of whispers and realization at the base
of it, and ice gathers, and the birds & fishes. But do not put yourself
out of this poem to feel because

In outspoken wakefulness, where hearts are gathered, first dark dark
meltings, then miraculous seeing – the length of a woman's love, or sky /
and birds swimming, as if out / an open window!
every moment of faith. But do not put your palm down to touch this in the
dust because

In outspoken darkness of forgotten hearts, where there's remembering and
no more fear. Dustiness of ice. Each bird dancing in the pool of / in the
clink of hearts. And fishes glow, their lids open / shut again. Tiny
reddened hearts. But do not think yourself out of this poem-dust to see
because

In the outspoken darkness of forgotten hearts / salutations, watching
everything, there is the world glows suddenly
again. Limbs sodden with love. Ice dust. Hearts read all the way to
Tehran. And realization at base of it where
hopes gather, winged as at the window.[*]

---

[*]Mahvash Sabet was imprisoned in the infamous Evin prison, Tehran, between 2008 and 2017, for her Bahá'í Faith.

Here
  for Peter Riley

Realizing how much the sea – that she is of me,
and I am of her – and the distance between
is too much. Or, one morning, a discovery:
        the vista is a wrong one?
but the fine grain,
not so much shape, but then where was
                the azure promise?

    Or: youth's like so many
sudden leaves upon a tree – blink
and soon the other side,
I mean what's through the tree,
is obvious.

        If you balance that way too long,   holding out,
you lose consciousness.

        Yet when you stretch your fingertips
           to sky. Bloom,
      and you might miss it.

In The Family Box

In the family box there was
no Xmas present – there
there was no Xmas
present in the family box.
In the care box
in the heart of cares
where Xxxs should have been
were missing care
of all those present pasts.
In the family.
Wound-care
wound round care-hearts
marked by not one X, not
even too, no
heart of present,
happily or past, but only
point of cares.
Precious present-box
into the Xmas heart. So full
of care & other thoughts –
fully. Not one mark
of passion or omission, only
wound-salt, very carefully,
& wrapped with careful
thought, but without
care & only much
point, but without heart –
felt. Only much past
without marking.
Only much pain
without ending.

The Verdict
for Kaia Sand & Carole Mirakove

The judge is very angry; the woman is very scared.
The judge has lots of power; the woman does not have power.
The judge appears emotional; the woman appears emotional.
The judge is being irrational; the woman is being rational.
The judge is veering off topic; the woman is sticking to the facts.
The judge is aggressive towards his questioners; the woman is polite towards her questioners.
The judge's story doesn't stand up to scrutiny; the woman's story stands up to scrutiny.
The judge's version has many holes; the woman's version does not have holes.
The judge doesn't drink out of control; the judge's friends recall him drinking out of control.
The judge has been in bar fights; the woman has not been in any bar fights.
The judge has never blacked out; have *you* ever blacked out?
The judge disputes going to those kinds of gatherings; the judge's diary records him going to those kinds of gatherings.
The judge has always viewed women with respect; his yearbook comments are being misinterpreted.
The judge's good name has been compromised for weeks; the woman's wellbeing has been compromised for decades.
The woman received therapy for the incident; the judge maintains the incident did not occur.
Attacks on the judge are politically motivated; attacks on the woman are par for the course.
The judge's job is to judge others; the woman's job is to understand conflict.
The judge does not like being judged himself; our daily jobs often become us.
The judge has the most conservative voting record on the D.C. Court, in every policy area, between 2003 and 2018.
The judge is a very public figure; the woman was 'terrified' to go public.
The judge has been subject to vociferous protests; the woman has received death threats and had to move homes.

Sixty-five female signatories who have known the judge 'for more than 35 years' assert that he has always 'behaved honorably and treated women with respect'; over one thousand alumnae of the woman's former school signed a letter saying that her accusation was 'all too consistent with stories we heard and lived'.

The judge fears his reputation is in tatters; the woman feared he would accidentally kill her.

The woman screamed out for help; the judge and his friend laughed.

The woman will never forget this happened; the judge may have convinced himself this never happened.

The judge agreed to testify on September 24, 2018; the woman asked that the FBI investigate the matter first.

The Senate Judiciary Committee Chair declined her request, instead giving her a deadline of September 21, 2018 to inform the Committee whether she intended to testify.

The judge's children pray for the woman; we don't know if the woman is a good Christian.

The president supported the judge; the president stated that 'you can do anything to a woman'.

The judge got elected to The Supreme Court; the woman disappeared from view.

Room On Fire [first Hollywood & now this]

You suck the bloom of your flirt,
        break each willing cherry plant. It is not enough
to say, but it is willing. Come down from there –
        because the other was too difficult, put up too much
intent. To match you somehow terror mutual-
        izing. I have taught you many warnings,
translated the most major explanations,
        warmed your metaphors even, spat out
the obvious, still no sympathy grows there. From the be-
        ginning sexual, not general de-
humaning. Not enough. Because the Gate to Art some-
        how Holy, the gate Her, Soul-Gate, some
& not whole, & It is Not-her if not Her, She
        is willing cherry break, & your eye camera, never
neutral. You take away
        Her, exposed, it is your Advertise.
Advise. How we all know
        endless growth, never full blossom how
ever. How we all experience. Except No. You don't
        remember, never grew –
a child: helpless at your body bursting
        ripped to seams, stupid head-less vomits
no Art only gone to seed to carry the next
        breed. Dumb container – like an empty building
for your party! Re-sounding symbol
        to be filled: The Big Idea You – or eaten by eyes
(notyou) or hissed at for feeding your new, too confusing
        (is it not sexual. Is it notnot
sexual. Because no head?) because we all
        grow up on those anti-bodies. Or
Walk through natural triangles? Try cultural rebirth

>Through triangle of fire. Where is natural?
Where is health? Is it only when You Idea. Try
>disappearing beneath cherry ground. When you come back
up for air everyone is not there, does forget. But
>triangle is still. Same empty cut. Same not-there.
Same On-Fire with same same notunderstanding.
>Culture notwithstanding.

5.11.18

Love, my love, is very delicate
Please do not snap its swan neck
Please do not pluck out its wings
Please do not remove its masses of feathers
(even those that stick in the throat)
Please do not not let it fly / swim
Please do not point your gun at it
(or keep sharp knives at the ready)
Please do not prepare a boiling pot
Please do not season a deep dish
Please do not set a timer to time
Please do not count the hours or minutes
Love cannot be perfect at the bell
Love cannot be tenderest to swallow
Not even sometimes sufficiently to try
Still, love, my love, is very delicate
If you know how to leave it alive.

No Title [Language is the House of Being]
for Cathy Wagner

There is no more room for language in the mud house: in it where she washes mud, every day, scrubbing until it falls from the ceiling and the walls cave in. Where she tends to all the animals and spits out fire. There is no jumping off point either. Now that she has responsibilities; muffled cheer around the centre piece; everyone holding their breath at Christmas and passing around cake crumbs. Where everything won't hold. Where it has to. Every little thing. Where they tend toward animals and, after that, probably the laughter; and the careless slaughter. Love carcasses. Then back to mud scrubbing. Scrubbing the mud, and so on. So much so that little light holes appear in the ceiling. Sky pokes around above, trying but not managing to come through. Shiny pinpricks. Remember to unhunch the shoulders. Remember balance. Remember breathing, and the mantra. Forget the mantra; no faith in it left. Forget words. No more words. No room left for them in the mud house. Where mud begets more mud and nothing but.

Two Lessons
for Denise Riley

1

Learn to love yourself, she said, and fuck them.
Footstep in the hallway, shadows echoing. Take hold
my palm and drag me there. Even the one that thinks so far –
I won't make it alone, I said. Retracing my steps,
the lost breadcrumbs. What country made you? Love
goes like that, she said, if you let it, tho sometimes
too recalls difference. Some god can tell the rest,
she said, there's no more why or less. Just have to press on
through intent, each reported sentiment. The air, I said,
might start getting lean. Just have to fall into it, toward
land, like the sea lets it. Formed by your own hands.
And that way is it, I said, heart-felt or flooded?

2

The backdrop was a secret
secret blue. There had been no
physical rain for ages illuminating
the pleasantness of the year
's flowers. There they still were
however waving. Even if far away
and in shadow. Even if you couldn't tell
them; the reason for which was
quite moving. And could always
have been read a different way. Any
way, your reading me about it now
doesn't make it any less amazing.

I'm Walking Away From You Now And I Can't

The arms that want to hold this moment, but they are too much stone,
& you are stationed underground, without a sign

> (and I'm scared that you do not love me
> & scared that you love me;
> I'm scared that I do not love you
> & scared that I love you).

Love – that just the most petrifying of things, since having a family,
since excuse me, where are you from, since I don't speak German,
could you say that in feeling?

Since the great Exterminating Angel took me
by your arms, shook us
down with peanut crumbs,
          declared itself a holy effigy.

Bluebottles

Still it kept bumping up against a shadow
of her own window.
and who put it there.
the swallow with the blue
bottle in its beak?*

*from Eleni Sikelianos, 'Bluebottle flies, blue light'

Victory Blossoms
on an anniversary

O you, most beloved of fifty-two different seasons, i lllll ya. Meh moi mich, to y, ya,
       youch – Us?
Between – is there not nothing wrong!
Yes! There is not nothing!
I mean: to belong (not the other way around)
Where are you home – again, or from? Your tie doesn't match the shoes – or is it belt –
       & I am wooed, woo, du, your tie – it shows where I am dreamt
But is it you!
Dreams speak to me, tell me not to be absurd,
Tell me not to want a husband – you, ya, tu.
Some people will always marry, let them tarry, under churchlight, till the moth dusts get
       them while we
Wonder on our knees & beg;
Hi! We are both so keen & new (/blue)
In slow snow light.
Red night, yellow night, what do people say?
Winning poem: 1. There are no answers
              2. Love is 'quite' strange
              3. Victory laurels are
for those who pay
& play & always say. But then they are to blame! But I love you –
       in writing – all the same.
And green is the colour of our love. And blue in summer.*
In the blossom seas or golden winter.
Y-O-U after one winter. Now two.
Y-O-U, do in the snow fall of a
Year – this victory –
I count it on my eyes & hair,
              it mouths us everywhere.

---

*'The dear earth everywhere blossoms in spring and grows green anew! Everywhere and forever blue is the horizon! ever … ever …' – Gustav Mahler, 'Abschied', *Das Lied von der Erde*

Out of Joint
for Aaron Kent & Ági Lehóczky

Lifelines in our hands
to grasp details of which
I am travelling past
snapshots of myself
travelling past
a simple graph
whatever sings
the difference. Planned
landslides are better
than... Listen,
I could tell
you about
nothing:
how to bite off
one's thumb in spite,*
bitten, repeated, blood
cutting around
the finite
vortex.
When we made up
this family
(out of scraps,
adjacent stories)
but when we have this
permanent rainbow –
smash the windows, let the rain off
this precious train
the one over all Europe.
Its new goal:
a stupid arrival.
Blood thumbs.

---

* 'And the continuance of their parents' rage'

Snow
for Daniel

This great surface
The expanse of which
This open thought
This half finished –
Not beyond
And yet beyond
Our being otherwise
This path towards
And falling weather even
As those steps lightly,
Lightly taken, blindly
Which we do not see
(the sky has more or less
them covered) on the way
To (more or less)
Where, softly, faith
Or non-implicitly precipitates
This binding ground
This heart forest
This solid coolness
This new music –
Which is always
New mind – and feel
(and has to be)
Which even now has ever
Just, but as the first time,
Permanently happened.

Author Biography

Emily Critchley is the author of fourteen poetry collections including *alphabet poem: for kids!* (Protoype, 2020), *Arrangements* (Shearsman Books, 2019) and *Ten Thousand Things* (Boiler House Press, 2018). She is the editor of *Out of Everywhere 2: Linguistically Innovative Poetry by Women in North America & the UK* (Reality Street, 2016) and co-editor of *#MeToo: A Poetry Collective* (Chicago Review, Summer 2018).

Critchley is Senior Lecturer in English and Creative Writing at the University of Greenwich. She lives with her daughter in London.

About Prototype

poetry / prose / interdisciplinary projects / anthologies

Creating new possibilities in the publishing of fiction and poetry through a flexible, interdisciplinary approach and the production of unique and beautiful books.

Prototype is an independent publisher working across genres and disciplines, committed to discovering and sharing work that exists outside the mainstream.

Each publication is unique in its form and presentation, and the aesthetic of each object is considered critical to its production.

Prototype strives to increase audiences for experimental writing, as the home for writers and artists whose work requires a creative vision not offered by mainstream literary publishers.

In its current, evolving form, Prototype consists of 4 strands of publications:

(type 1 — poetry)
(type 2 — prose)
(type 3 — interdisciplinary projects)
(type 4 — anthologies) including an annual anthology of new work, *PROTOTYPE*.

( )   (   )